ALTERNATOR
BOOKS™

MISSION
RUBY

SHEELA
PREUITT

Lerner Publications ◆ Minneapolis

TO DUSTIN, FOR ALL THE
FEEDBACK AND SUPPORT

Lerner Publications Company
An imprint of Lerner Publishing Group, Inc.
241 First Avenue North
Minneapolis, MN 55401 USA

For reading levels and more information, look up this title at
www.lernerbooks.com.

Main body text set in Aptifer Slab LT Pro.
Typeface provided by Linotype.

Library of Congress Cataloging-in-Publication Data

Names: Preuitt, Sheela, author.
Title: Mission Ruby / Sheela Preuitt.
Description: Minneapolis : Lerner Publications, [2020] | Series: Mission:
    code (alternator books) | Audience: Age 8–12. | Audience: Grade 4 to
    6. | Includes bibliographical references and index.
Identifiers: LCCN 2018059329 (print) | LCCN 2018061639 (ebook) |
    ISBN 9781541556409 (eb pdf) | ISBN 9781541555921 (lb : alk. paper) |
    ISBN 9781541573765 (pb : alk. paper)
Subjects: LCSH: Ruby (Computer program language)—Juvenile
    literature.
Classification: LCC QA76.73.R83 (ebook) | LCC QA76.73.R83 P74 2020
    (print) | DDC 005.13/3—dc23

LC record available at https://lccn.loc.gov/2018059329

Manufactured in the United States of America
1-46048-43464-4/24/2019

CONTENTS

To download the solutions for the Your Mission: Code It! activities, visit http://qrs.lernerbooks.com/Ruby. The coding activities in this book do not require you to download Ruby. However, if you want to use Ruby on your desktop, download it from https://www.ruby-lang.org/en /downloads/. Always seek the help of an adult when downloading files from the internet.

INTRODUCTION
THE
HISTORY
OF RUBY

Interested in creating video games or websites? The Ruby programming language is a great way to get started!

A programmer named Yukihiro (Matz) Matsumoto created Ruby in 1995. He wanted to make a high-level language that is easy to learn and use but powerful enough to perform complex tasks.

Since Ruby was invented, programmers have used it to create video streaming and social networking websites, including Hulu and Twitter. Let's see how they did it!

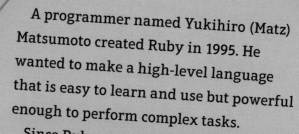

Ruby creator Yukihiro Matsumoto taught himself how to code while he was in school.

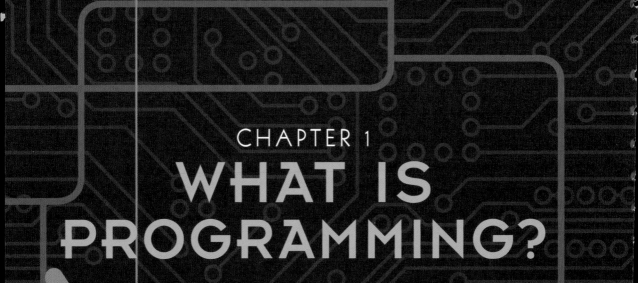

CHAPTER 1
WHAT IS
PROGRAMMING?

There are many **programming languages** today, such as JavaScript, Ruby, and Python. Each language has its own **syntax** of words, punctuation, and rules about how to use them.

You can write Ruby **programs** using the Ruby syntax. This works by typing lines of code and then **executing** them. The computer follows the instructions and does the task you want it to do. Often it will **print**, or display, something on the screen.

As you practice coding, it will get easier to read and write it—just as learning a spoken language does.

Sometimes when you type a Ruby program, you might make a mistake. If this happens, Ruby will print an error message on the screen. Don't get discouraged if you get this message. All programmers make mistakes. Usually the error message will tell you where in the code the error is located, as well as what type of error it is. You can then fix the error and execute the program again.

Are you ready to see Ruby in action?

With the help of an adult, open a web browser and go to
https://repl.it/repls/FormalGlaringCoin. When the website
loads, you will see three columns. The middle column should
have three lines of code:

```
puts "Hello, friend. What is your name?"
friendsName = gets.chomp
puts "Nice to meet you, #{friendsName}.
Let's learn Ruby!"
```

Click the green Run button at the top of the page. What do you
see in the dark column on the right? Type your name into the
dark column, and
press Enter on your
keyboard. Now what
do you see?

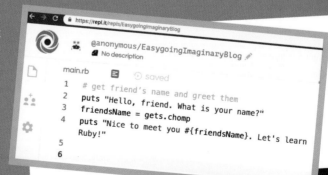

CHAPTER 2
DIVE INTO THE DATA

PROGRAMS HELP STORE, FIND, AND USE DATA. Data is any piece of information we want to keep track of or do something with.

Ruby has two basic types of data, numbers and strings. Numbers are just like the numbers you use in math class. You can use both whole numbers and decimals. *String* is another way of saying "text." Use quotes to enclose a bunch of characters, and they become a string.

There are many ways to use or change data. For example, you can use Ruby as a calculator:

```
2 + 2
=> 4
3 * 6
=> 18
```

You can also use *.even?* to check if a number is even or odd.

```
22.even?
=>true
33.even?
=>false
```

Or you can use *between?* to ask if a number is between two other numbers.

```
22.between?(5,30)
=>true
44.between?(10,40)
=>false
```

Ruby lets you do interesting things with strings too. You can add them . . .

```
"I am a " + "string in Ruby "
+ "joined together with " + "the
plus sign!"
=> I am a string in Ruby joined
together with the plus sign!
```

. . . or multiply them!

```
"Hello! " * 3
=> Hello! Hello! Hello!
```

One of the coolest things you can do is reverse all the characters in a string:

```
"Howdy!".reverse
=>!ydwoH
```

Besides numbers and strings, there are other data types, including symbols, Booleans, and a special **value** called nil. Boolean data can have only one of two values: true or false. And *nil* means "nothing"! You use nil when you want a value to be empty.

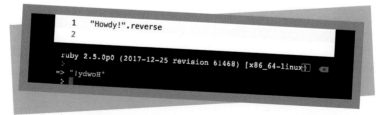

This screenshot shows what the code will look like on your screen.

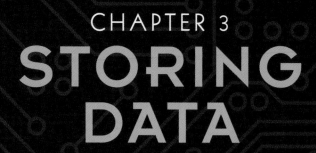

CHAPTER 3
STORING DATA

NOW THAT YOU KNOW ABOUT THE DIFFERENT TYPES OF DATA, YOU CAN ORGANIZE THEM INTO LISTS, GROUPS, AND EVEN DICTIONARIES. Organizing data will make typing and reading your code much easier.

Another way to make your code easy to read is to use indents. Indents don't change how your code works, so they're very useful for organizing the lines of code. Professional programmers use indents for this purpose.

A **variable** is like a container that can hold one thing at a time. You can store something to reuse it later as many times as you want. Variables can hold any type of data, including numbers, strings, and Booleans. For example, you can create a variable for your street address:

```
myAddress = "123 Pine Street,
Some City, Any State, USA 99999."
```

If you want to use this address in your program, just type the variable *myAddress* instead of typing the whole thing.

```
1 myAddress = "123 Pine Street, Some City, Any State, USA 99999."
```

Ruby often uses colors to show each part of the code.

It is helpful to name your variables something that is easy to remember. In Ruby, variable names cannot begin with numbers or contain spaces, symbols, or punctuation. The variable name *my Cat's Name* will cause errors. Also, remember that Ruby is case sensitive, meaning that *myCatsName* is different from *mycatsname*.

One thing you can do with variables is compare them to see if one is bigger than or equal to the other. You can do this with comparison operators. These comparison operators result in either *true* or *false*. In the table below, the letters *x* and *y* are variables. The letter *x* equals 100 and the letter *y* equals 200.

Operator	Operation	Example	Result
==	Equal to	x == y	false
!=	Not equal to	x != y	true
>	Greater than	x > y	false
<	Less than	x < y	true
>=	Greater than or equal to	x >= 100	true
<=	Less than or equal to	y <= 200	true

Coding an array is a fast way to get organized.

An **array** is like a list. It is a handy way to store a bunch of values in a single place. For example, let's say you are making a list of snacks to serve at your birthday party. You could code it like this:

```
mySnackList = ["carrots",
"strawberry mice", "ants on
a log", "crackers and cheese",
"grapes", "cucumber sandwiches"]
```

To access an individual item in this list, use an **array index**. An array index always starts at zero. In *mySnackList*, the first item, carrots, is item number 0. Use square brackets with the array index inside it to access that item. For example, to see what item is at index position 0, 1, or 3, use the command *puts*, as shown below.

```
puts mySnackList[0]
=>carrots
puts mySnackList[1]
=>strawberry mice
puts mySnackList[3]
=>crackers and cheese
```

You can fill an array with numbers, strings, Booleans, and even other arrays.

Let's say you need to study for a Spanish test. It would be nice to have a simple English-to-Spanish dictionary to look up your vocabulary words. In Ruby, you can create that dictionary using a **hash**.

Flipping through a physical dictionary takes a lot of time. Speed up the process with a hash.

Hashes look up values based on **keys**. In this example, an English word is the key and the Spanish word is the value.

```
1  mySpanishWords = {
2      "cat" => "gato",
3      "dog" => "perro",
4      "hello" => "hola",
5      "goodbye" => "adios",
6      "please" => "por favor",
7      "thank you" => "gracias",
8      "house" => "casa"
9  }
10
```

A Ruby hash should be typed as in the example above.

If you want to look up only one value at a time, give the hash the correct key. For example, if you don't remember the Spanish word for "dog," you could look it up in your hash:

```
puts mySpanishWords["dog"]
=>perro
```

You can also have numbers, Booleans, and other data types in a hash. Let's say you learned some new words in Spanish class and want to add them to your dictionary. Simply assign a new *key* and *value* using square brackets.

```
mySpanishWords[1] = "uno"
mySpanishWords[2] = "dos"
```

Check the result:

```
puts mySpanishWords
=>{"cat" => "gato", "dog" =>
"perro", "hello" => "hola",
"goodbye" => "adios", "please"
=> "por favor", "thank you" =>
"gracias", "house" => "casa",
1=> "uno", 2=> "dos"}
```

Now studying will be a breeze!

CODE IT!

Create a hash for ten US state capitals. Remember to press the green Run button at the top of the screen to execute your code.

1. Code a hash called *stateCapitals* that has the name of a state for each key and the state capital as the value. For example, Oregon's capital is Salem, so that would look like `{"Oregon" => "Salem"}`. Add nine more states and capitals to the hash.

2. Use *puts* to print your hash. Make sure it looks how you expect it to.

3. Ask your parent for the name of one of the states in your hash. Use your hash to look up the state capital. Did your hash get it right?

CHAPTER 4

CONDITIONALS, LOOPS, AND METHODS

EVERY DAY, YOU MAKE MANY

```
1  if feelSick == true
2      puts "Stay home and rest"
3  else
4      puts "Go to school!"
5  end
6
```

When you have multiple conditions, you can use
the *if*, *elsif*, and *else* keywords. You can use as many
elsif keywords as needed.

```
1  if testScore >= 90
2      puts "You get an A!"
3  elsif testScore.between?(80, 89)
4      puts "You get a B"
5  elsif testScore.between?(70, 79)
6      puts "You get a C"
7  else
8      puts "You get an F"
9  end
10
```

To repeat a certain program over and over, you can use loops. There are two basic types of loops. The first type continues doing something as long as a condition is true and stops doing it when the condition becomes false. This is the while-loop, as it uses the keywords *while* and *end*.

A number-guessing game is one place you might use this kind of loop. In this game, a player tries to guess a secret number. If they guess wrong, they can try again. Once they get it right, the loop ends.

```
@anonymous/EasygoingImaginaryBlog
No description

main.rb                    history

1   secretNumberToGuess = 7
2   playersGuess = 0
3   while (playersGuess.to_i != secretNumberToGuess)
4     puts "Guess a number between 1 and 10:"
5     playersGuess = gets.chomp
6     if (playersGuess.to_i == secretNumberToGuess)
7     puts "You guessed it! The number is #
      {secretNumberToGuess}."
8     puts "Good-bye!"
9     break
10    else
11    puts "Sorry, guess again..."
12    secretNumberToGuess = rand(1..10)
13    playersGuess = 0
14    end
15  end
```

This program is one way to code a number-guessing game. Can you see what all the different lines of code do?

The second type of loop is called an *iterator*. The job of an iterator is to go through an array of items and do the same action with each item.

There are many different iterators. One common iterator is the keyword *each*. If you wanted Ruby to write out the colors of the rainbow, you could first create an array that contains all the colors and then use the *each* iterator.

```
colorsOfRainbow = [
  "red", "orange", "yellow",
  "green", "blue", "indigo",
  "violet"
]
colorsOfRainbow.each do |color|
  puts color
end
```

Programmers can define a set of instructions once, and then use it many times, whenever they need to. In Ruby, a set of instructions like this is called a **method**. Methods use the *def* and *end* keywords.

Now that the power of programming is in your hands, keep practicing your Ruby skills. With enough practice, you'll be able to join the ranks of programmers who work on scientific experiments, social media websites, and video games. Let's get coding!

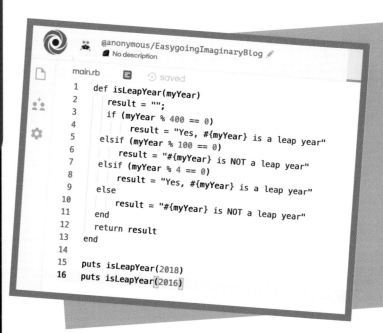

```ruby
@anonymous/EasygoingImaginaryBlog
No description

main.rb          saved
1    def isLeapYear(myYear)
2        result = "";
3        if (myYear % 400 == 0)
4            result = "Yes, #{myYear} is a leap year"
5        elsif (myYear % 100 == 0)
6            result = "#{myYear} is NOT a leap year"
7        elsif (myYear % 4 == 0)
8            result = "Yes, #{myYear} is a leap year"
9        else
10            result = "#{myYear} is NOT a leap year"
11        end
12        return result
13    end
14
15    puts isLeapYear(2018)
16    puts isLeapYear(2016)
```

This method checks if a year is a leap year or not. Use it as an example to help you with the Your Mission: Code It! activity on the next page.

A palindrome is a word or phrase that looks the same forward and backward. Your mission is to create a palindrome checker.

1. Ask for a word from a friend. Turn the word into a string to use in your code.

2. Reverse the string, and then check whether the reversed string matches the original string.

3. If they match, have Ruby say that the word is a palindrome. If they do not match, have Ruby say it is not a palindrome.

GLOSSARY

array: a list of values

array index: a number that tells you where an item is in an array

conditional statement: a line in code that tells a computer to do different things depending on true or false conditions

executing: telling a computer to run a program or code

hash: a program that lets you look up values based on keys

keys: a word that looks up a value in a hash

method: an action done to a value, variable, array, or hash

print: to display on a screen

programming languages: words and symbols that tell computers how to understand programs

programs: instructions that tell a computer what to do

syntax: the words and symbols a programming language uses, as well as the rules about how to use them

value: a single piece of data that is stored in variables, arrays, and hashes

variable: a programming container that stores a single value at a time

FURTHER INFORMATION

The Definitive Ruby Tutorial for Complete Beginners
https://www.rubyguides.com/ruby-tutorial/

Haupt, Christopher. *Ruby for Kids for Dummies.* Hoboken, NJ: John Wiley & Sons, 2016.

Learning Ruby: From Zero to Hero
https://medium.freecodecamp.org/learning -ruby-from-zero-to-hero-90ad4eecc82d

Learn Ruby
https://www.learnrubyonline.org/

Preuitt, Sheela. *Mission JavaScript.* Minneapolis: Lerner Publications, 2020.

Weinstein, Eric. *Ruby Wizardry: An Introduction to Programming for Kids.* San Francisco: No Starch, 2015.

INDEX

PHOTO ACKNOWLEDGMENTS

Various screenshots by Sheela Preuit. Additional images: Mathias/flickr (CC BY-SA 2.0), p. 5; JGI/Tom Grill/Getty Images, p. 7; grebeshkovmaxim/Shutterstock.com, p. 8; Iamtheshutter/Shutterstock.com, p. 16; Stock-Asso/Shutterstock.com, p. 18; Stuwdamdorp/Alamy Stock Photo, p. 20; Cover and interior design elements: HuHu/Shutterstock.com (runner); Vankad/Shutterstock.com (circuits); Bro Studio/Shutterstock.com (circular pattern); Leremy/Shutterstock.com (figures).